Tom Cooper and Jen McGregor

THE GLASGOW POISONER

A New Musical

Salamander Street

PLAYS

First published in 2025 by Salamander Street Ltd., a Wordville imprint. (info@salamanderstreet.com).

The Glasgow Poisoner © Tom Cooper and Jen McGregor, 2025

ISBN: 9781068233456

10 9 8 7 6 5 4 3 2 1

Further copies of this publication can be purchased from
www.salamanderstreet.com

Wordville

H.R. MILLAR

INTRODUCTION BY JEN MCGREGOR

To say that I've known the Madeleine Smith story for years would be an understatement. I first encountered her case in a book of Scottish crime stories when I was 15 or 16 and she immediately piqued my interest. My parents, both Glaswegian, only encouraged me by telling me about Glasgow's 'square mile of murder' and the time my Grandad lived in a rented attic room on Blythswood Square which he claimed was haunted by an Egyptian mummy. Later in my teens, towards the end of a romance conducted largely by email, my interest took on a new dimension (though rest assured all parties involved were alive and well and, to the best of my knowledge, still are!)

I devoured everything I could find about Madeleine—trial records, books, graphic novels, even the David Lean film which wasn't available in the UK in the early 2000s. I still prize the DVD I tracked down, complete with unremovable Dutch subtitles. In 2012, shortly after graduating from drama school, I commissioned a brilliant playwright of my acquaintance to write a play about Madeleine for me to direct. The resulting work, Fiona McDonald's *I Promise I Shall Not Play Billiards*, had an Edinburgh Fringe run at the Royal Scots Club on Abercromby Place, formerly the home of Madeleine's legal counsel, John Inglis QC. It's fair to say that this story has been a constant presence throughout my life.

In 2024 I made my writing debut at A Play, A Pie And A Pint with a play called *Who Pays the Piper*, directed by Tom Cooper. We were keen to work together again, and Tom told me there was a musical he'd like to make and thought I might be the person he needed to write the book. We met to talk about it, and he got as far as "On Blythswood Square" before I yelled "MADELEINE" and proceeded to infodump for a solid half hour before I drew breath and Tom got a word in to confirm that yes, the subject matter was the infamous Miss Smith.

Of course I was on board, but I had one condition—I did not want to do a straightforward retelling in which we decided the question of Madeleine's guilt or innocence. What interested me was the question of the Not Proven verdict. It's a legal phenomenon that goes back to Ancient Rome but by Madeleine's time was found only in Scotland, and still exists. At the time of writing there's a bill going through the Scottish Parliament which proposes to abolish it. The question of whether we should or not is one I'll leave to people who understand it better than I do, but in dramatic terms I found it an interesting starting point for considering how we think about justice and how important the things that happen in the grey area between innocence and guilt can be.

On the one hand, perhaps it makes sense to have a verdict available which acknowledges that what a court assesses isn't really innocence but evidence. In Madeleine's case it was impossible to determine that she and Emile actually met on the night he ingested the arsenic. She had always been haphazard in putting dates on letters. When her correspondence was found in Emile's desk, some of the envelopes had multiple letters stuffed into them so that it was difficult to date them by postmark. She didn't keep the letters he sent her, so dates couldn't be worked out by comparing them. No witnesses saw them in the same place, which is perhaps unsurprising for a secret affair. Yet she did have arsenic in her possession, she certainly had a motive, and Emile certainly did die of arsenic poisoning. If he was murdered by Madeleine then of course her walking free was unjust to her victim. But Emile had a history of boasting that he took arsenic recreationally, and he was believed to have attempted suicide over a breakup before, so the possibility that he poisoned himself certainly belonged in the mix. It's tricky enough set of possibilities to present in an hour-long musical—I can only imagine what it would have been like to consider all of this as a jury member knowing that a person's life hung in the balance.

My next question was what we were going to do about Emile. Whereas we have extensive records of Madeleine's side of the correspondence, we don't have Emile's. She burned his letters. He only kept copies of a few, and their content is damning—for instance, he kept the one where he asks why she didn't bleed after supposedly losing her virginity to him. Considering his habit of threatening to show all the letters to her father and Madeleine's frantic attempts to get them back in the final days of their relationship, it's hard to see this as an innocent souvenir. It seems very close to the present-day phenomenon of people keeping an ex's nudes for revenge porn. But however unfavourable a light Emile's own writing paints him in, I didn't want to make him a one-dimensional villain.

I found I was curious about his status as a man who didn't come from great wealth—not grinding poverty either, but a standard of living that saw him lodging in a boarding house in his mid-30s without much career progression either behind him or ahead of him. He had made at least one (possibly two) previous attempts to marry into wealth before, so it seems reasonable to suppose that Madeleine's rich family appealed to him and informed his unwillingness to elope with her. Madeleine was clearly game—her letters frequently show her trying to work out how to get the banns read (a custom of announcing upcoming marriages in church for three weeks prior to the actual wedding) without her family finding out. She considers running away to Edinburgh, London, even Lima... but every time Emile puts on the brakes, concerned that without her father's consent he will find himself as broke as before, but this time with a wife to support. I wanted to capture that sense that this is a high stakes game for Emile, and that perhaps it's fair enough for him to be a fortune hunter in a society which would think nothing of Madeleine doing the same. It's his other behaviours that damn him, not his desire for a comfortable life. (It's also worth noting that Madeleine's father had married up—although he was professionally successful, it was her mother who came from money!)

Perhaps Emile's worries about Madeleine being cut off financially were unfounded—after all, her family supported her when she was arrested and tried for murder. They paid for the finest legal defence available, so perhaps they would have tried to style out a scandalous marriage after all.

On the subject of Madeleine's marriages, there's one figure I was sorry to have to minimise and that's William Minnoch. In addition to being Madeleine's acceptable fiancé, he was the Smiths' next door neighbour and was willing to stand by Madeleine when she was arrested. They parted ways after the trial, once the sexual nature of her relationship with Emile had been revealed, but he comes across as quite sweet in her correspondence with him and I'd have liked to explore his thoughts and responses to the strange situation he found himself in.

Likewise Madeleine's younger sister Janet, with whom she shared not only that basement bedroom but the actual bed. Likewise Madeleine's servant Christina Haggart, and Emile's friend Mary Perry, both of whom acted as go-betweens for the lovers at various times. Likewise the Smith family's earlier residences, including the house on India Street where Madeleine let Emile in via the front door—shocking! Likewise Emile working at the Botanic Gardens, where industrial arsenic was available for the taking. Likewise Madeleine's further adventures—her life in London where she mixed with artists and socialists, her possible emigration to New York where she knocked a couple of decades off her age (giving 1857, the year of her trial, as the year of her birth instead), all the reported sightings of her, the time a newspaper in Stirling falsely reported her death in a carriage accident because it was a slow news day. Fine, I lied, there's a ton of material I'd have loved to include! It's always the case with condensing historical material into an hour-long show, there's so much that has to be simplified for clarity. Of course, if anyone wants to fund a real-time reenactment to be performed over two and a half years, in the very locations in which it all happened, I'll be happy to collaborate—but you can write that funding application, not me!

I hope the musical provides a fun introduction to Madeleine's story for those who don't already know about it, and a satisfyingly twisty engagement with it for those who do. I hope Plume's dilemma feels recognisable not only to those interested in this particular case, but to anyone who has ever been fascinated by a true crime story, struggled to puzzle out why people behave the way they do, or had a complex relationship with rules.

Jen McGregor
2025

INTRODUCTION BY TOM COOPER

A Play A Pie and a Pint is extraordinary. Not only are they the most prolific producer of new plays in the UK (by some distance), they've also long been great encouragers of musical theatre. The team understands that musicals can be and do a limitless variety of things. And brilliantly, they've never hemmed themselves into a set way of thinking about what a musical might be, might look like, might sound like or could be about.

Like Jen, I first read about Madeleine Smith in a book of Glasgow crime stories (99p from The Works). It was the unsolved-ness of the whole thing that made it stick in my mind. The recorded historical facts could be interpreted in multiple ways, supporting a number of possible narratives of what might have happened. And within each of these possible narratives were strong, heady emotional drives: a very young girl in the flush of first love, dealing with the pressure of parental and societal expectation, and suddenly grieving, only to then be accused of something horrific. Or stuck in so much fear that murder really did seem the only way forward to her. Or a man playing the high-stakes game of trying to secure a financially advantageous marriage, only to be girl-boss-beaten at his own game. Or all the other possibilities. Theatre would help us stack layers of verbal and visual information into each version quickly, with music adding varied rhythmic, melodic and harmonic information too, all affecting different parts of the brain. This felt like an invitation to play with a range of musical styles.

Madeleine's own time period was an influence. I dug around in Victorian music hall: simple-seeming comic ditties, beautifully constructed. As a curious mirror to these, church hymn music from the period offered similar musical structures, with more harmonic weight, and often a satisfying, stately sweetness. A point of triangulation with these is the work of Arthur Sullivan, who wrote both for the hymnal and the music hall, as well as his operettas and one opera, though it's his parlour songs that I find compelling, and which I've tried to lean into.

In terms of musical theatre influences, our particular blend of the dark and the playful probably owes something to Hollman and Kotis' *Urinetown*. And, in putting a murder-musical in front of a pie-eating audience, it felt we couldn't not try and give small aspirational nods, at points, towards Sondheim's masterful *Sweeney Todd*.

The flexibility of the concept allowed other flavours into the score too. In the version of the story where Madeleine kills Emile as the only way she sees out of her predicament, we were excited to explore something much more contemporary. What if the kind of lovelorn, bile-spitting female pop-punk song that the charts are currently full of were to go as far as actually murdering the ex-boyfriend? Is that the point were the singing character would lose the empathy of the audience, or could we take them with us?

We're grateful to PPP for giving us a deadline, as well as for Brian Noble's dramaturgical support, and for allowing us to have the fabulous Sam Macdonald as an on-stage musical director as well as arranger and song-dramaturg. It's been a joy to collaborate with Jen and Sam and our wonderful cast and the PPP team to put this small but huge and knotty story on stage.

Tom Cooper
2025

ACKNOWLEDGEMENTS

We'd like to thank:

Susan Taylor of the Special Collections department at the Mitchell Library, Glasgow, who let us view their collection of Madeleine-related materials, including thirteen of Madeleine's original letters.

Brian Logan, and all at *A Play, A Pie and a Pint*.

Sarah Johnson and Jane Hensey at The Royal Conservatoire of Scotland.

The Glasgow Poisoner was first produced at A Play, A Pie And A Pint on Monday 22nd September 2025 with the following cast and creative team:

Plume	**Morgan E. Ross**
Madeleine	**Chiara Sparkes**
Emile	**David Joseph Healy**
Composer, Lyricist & Co-Director	**Tom Cooper**
Writer, Lyricist & Co-Director	**Jen McGregor**
Musical Director & Arranger	**Samuel Macdonald**
Set and Costume Design	**Heather Currie**
Choreographer	**Hannah Docherty**
Lighting Design	**Ross Nurney**

A piano-vocal score of the songs for *The Glasgow Poisoner* is available from Tom Cooper. Please contact him via his website: www.tomcooper.uk

CAST

Morgan E. Ross | Plume

Morgan E. Ross is delighted to be making their professional acting debut in *The Glasgow Poisoner* at A Play, A Pie and A Pint. A recent graduate with First Class Honours in Acting, Morgan has previously collaborated with Framework Theatre and Aberdeen Performing Arts. Passionate about musical theatre, he is thrilled to be fulfilling a long-held dream with this production.

Chiara Sparkes | Madeleine

Chiara trained at The Dance School of Scotland and Royal Conservatoire of Scotland. Her theatre credits include *Rollers Forever* (Pavilion Theatre, Glasgow); *So Long, Wee Moon* (Braw Clan); *Tally's Blood* (Scottish Tour); *Mamma Mia!* (UK/ International Tour); *Bridezilla and the Orchid of Sin* (A Play, Pie and a Pint); *Glasgow Girls* (RAW Material UK/Ireland Tour 2019 & National Theatre of Scotland/Pachamama UK Tour 2017); *The Snow Queen* (Noisemaker/Dundee Rep); *The Yellow on the Broom* (Dundee Rep); *Eddie & The Slumber Sisters* (Catherine Wheels/National Theatre of Scotland, Scottish Tour); *Mother Goose, Sleeping Beauty* (Ayr Gaiety); *Thread* (Kick the Door); *Robin Hood* (Cumbernauld Theatre). TV/Screen Credits: 'Scotland is Open' for Scotland is Now Global Campaign (Forest of Black); *The Kids Are Alt Right* (Braw Clan); *The Famous Grouse* (Greenroom Films); *Logan High* (Chalkboard/BBC). She is also co-director of Drive Official, producing events around Scotland.

David Joseph Healy | Emile

David is an actor and singer from Glasgow. He is a graduate of the Royal Conservatoire of Scotland. Recent performances include *The Great Gatsby* (Roman Theatre of Verulamium), *35mm* (Phoenix Arts Club), *A Little Night Music* (Assembly Rooms) and *Fountain of You* (Assembly Rooms).

CREATIVE TEAM

Tom Cooper | Composer & Lyricist

Tom Cooper is a director based in Glasgow, working across plays, musical theatre and opera. For A Play A Pie and a Pint he directed Jen McGregor's play *Who Pays the Piper*, and Shonagh Murray's musical *Armour: a herstory of the Scottish Bard*, which toured to the Traverse and Ayr Gaiety.

His other recent directing includes *The 25th Annual Putnam County Spelling Bee* (Royal Conservatoire of Scotland); *A Little Night Music* and *Big Fish* (RCS at Assembly Rooms, Edinburgh Fringe); *Gianni Schicchi* (Opera Bohemia, Scottish Tour); *La Traviata* (UK tour); *Part of the Picture* (also as writer, Pleasance, Edinburgh); Brecht's *The Visions of Simone Machard* (Hackney Empire and tour); *A Midsummer Night's Dream* (Blenheim Palace Gardens); *Stefano Benni's Astraroth* and the devised *L'Antologia di Spoon River* (Rapallo Festival, Italy); N. C. Hunter's play *A Day by the Sea* and the UK premiere of Adam Guettel's song cycle *Myths and Hymns* (Finborough Theatre, London).

Tom was an assistant director for the Young Vic Theatre, Opera North and English National Opera. He has been a member of the BML musical theatre writing workshop, the MMD Scottish MT writers' lab, and the Royal Court Young Writers' Programme. He is a part-time Lecturer in Musical Theatre at the Royal Conservatoire of Scotland.

Jen McGregor | Book Writer & Lyricist

Jen McGregor is an award-winning writer, dramaturg and director. Recent credits include *Who Pays the Piper* (A Play, A Pie and A Pint), *The Premorial* (Birds of Paradise/Perth Theatre), *Ghost Stories* (Pitlochry Festival Theatre), *HallucinoJen* (SMHAF), *HomoSapien* (Emma Ruse Productions) and *A Brief History of Neurodivergence* (Fiona Moon). Her play *Heaven Burns* won the 2018 ART Award.

Jen's first libretto, for Amble Skuse's chamber opera *Divergent Sounds*, debuted at the Southbank Centre in 2023 with the City of London Sinfonia. Her second, *Heaven Burns*, is in development with composer Sarah Ann Marze and received support from Second Movement in 2024.

Jen's work explores themes of self-invention, death fear/death drive, and finding your place in a world in which you don't easily fit.

Samuel Macdonald | Musical Director & Arranger

Samuel Macdonald is a musical director, pianist and composer/lyricist based in Glasgow. They are a graduate of the University of Cambridge and the Royal Conservatoire of Scotland. In the past year they have been music supervisor and arranger for new musicals across the UK, including workshops for Wildfire Season and Polly, and the 2024 Edinburgh Fringe production of *Savoy! Everybody's Doing It*, for which they also contributed music and lyrics. They are a co-founder of Matchstick Productions, a company dedicated to producing new original musicals in Scotland.

The Glasgow Poisoner

A New Musical

book and lyrics by Jen McGregor

music and lyrics by Tom Cooper

CHARACTERS

Madeleine Hamilton Smith
(1835-1921) society belle and possible poisoner

Pierre Emile L'Angelier
(1823-1857) gardener, clerk and fortune-hunter

Plume
an aspiring pamphleteer

SCENE 1.

PLUME's study—a chaotic little room containing a desk and a piano. The desk is covered with papers, so are the walls. Some of these papers are drafts and copies of PLUME's self-penned pamphlets, some are copies of letters that passed between MADELEINE and EMILE, some are scribbled notes pinned haphazardly together. PLUME is alone in the space, but this doesn't prevent him conjuring up his imagined companions—MADELEINE, EMILE and the MUSICIAN who sits at the piano accompanying PLUME's thoughts.

SONG 1: PENNY DREADFUL

PLUME: WE HOPE YOU ALL ENJOYED YOUR PIES
WATCH AND YOU CAN FEAST YOUR EYES
ON TALES OF WOE AND TALES OF FEAR
FROM YOUR FAVOURITE PAMPHLETEER

HER FAMILY LIVED JUST OVER THERE
AT NUMBER SEVEN, BLYTHSWOOD SQUARE
MADELEINE SMITH THE ELDEST DAUGHTER
SOCIETY BELLE, THOUGH MANY THOUGHT HER
CHARACTER WAS QUITE UNIQUE
SHE HAD… AN INDEPENDENT STREAK

IT'S A PENNY DREADFUL STORY
A GIRL FROM BLYTHSWOOD SQUARE
MEETS A DODGY FOREIGN FELLOW
HAS A CLANDESTINE AFFAIR

IT'S A PENNY DREADFUL STORY
SENSATION THROUGH-AND-THROUGH
A PENNY DREADFUL STORY
AND EVERY WORD IS TRUE.

MADELEINE in the courtroom, standing trial. EMILE delights in reading out the indictment.

EMILE: Madeleine Hamilton Smith, now or lately a prisoner in the Prison of Glasgow, you are indicted and accused of wickedly and feloniously administering a quantity of arsenic to Pierre Emile L'Angelier, now deceased, on 22nd of March eighteen hundred and fifty seven, in consequence thereof he suffered severe illness and did die, and was thus murdered by you.

PLUME: Prisoner at the bar. You have heard the indictment read. How do you plead? Guilty or not guilty?

Music stops.

MADELEINE: Not guilty.

Music continues.

PLUME: A PENNY DREADFUL STORY
READY-MADE FOR ME
TELLING TALES OF MURDER
IS MY SPECIALITY
A PENNY DREADFUL STORY
SENSATION THROUGH-AND-THROUGH
A PENNY DREADFUL STORY
AND EVERY WORD IS TRUE.

To start at the beginning. Madeleine Hamilton Smith, living in her father's house at Blythswood Square, Glasgow...

EMILE: GEORGIAN TERRACE, VERY PRETTY
LOVELY CORNER OF THE CITY

PLUME: ...is the tender age of 18.

MADELEINE: WE'RE AS PRIVELEGED AS YOU'D EXPECT
MY DADDY IS AN ARCHITECT.

I'VE JUST FINISHED FINISHING-SCHOOL IN SURREY.
ONE DAY I'LL FIND A HUSBAND
BUT I'M NOT IN ANY HURRY.

PLUME: Part One! On a spring day on Sauchiehall Street...

MADELEINE: LOOKING FOR A SATIN BONNET.

PLUME: ...a chance encounter! He's young(ish), mid-30s, impoverished, alive...

EMILE: (*offering her a rose*) Madamoiselle, you have dropped a flower.

MADELEINE: I wasn't carrying any /...   oh!

They exchange a long, meaningful look—music holds—he bows, she takes the flower.

EMILE: A pink rose for a pink rose. Au revoir, Mademoiselle Smith.

Music continues.

PLUME: How did he know who she was... ?

MADELEINE: I'm the daughter of one of Glasgow's leading families. He could've asked pretty much anyone.

PLUME: Part Two! The secret correspondence.
In nineteenth century Scotland, we write letters. Courtesy of Glasgow's penny post service—delivery within the hour for just a penny a letter!

PLUME picks up a copy of MADELEINE's first letter.

PLUME: Undated letter. We apologise for the lack of specificity, but it must have been Candlemas and Whitsun of 1855.

My dear Emile, I do not feel as if I were writing to you for the first time. Though our intercourse has been very short, yet we have become as familiar friends. Long may we continue so.

Rest assured I shall not mention to anyone that you have written me. I know from experience that the world is not lenient in its observations. But I do not care for the world's remarks so long as my own heart tells me I'm doing nothing wrong.

The MUSICIAN strikes a note on the piano—a notification that there's a letter for EMILE.

EMILE reads it, silently, as MADELEINE's missives intensify.

PLUME: 29th April 1855.

MADELEINE: DEAREST EMILE.

PLUME: 30th April.

MADELEINE: MY DEAR ONE.

PLUME: 1st May.

MADELEINE: MOST BELOVED.

PLUME: 2nd May.

MADELEINE: MY OWN MOST BELOVED.

PLUME: 2nd May.

MADELEINE: MY OWN, MY DEAREST, MY KINDEST.

PLUME: Later again on 2nd May.

MADELEINE: DARLING BELOVED, DEARLY BELOVED EMILE.

PLUME: Part Three: A Planned Elopement!

MADELEINE: MY OWN DEAR LOVE OF A SWEETHEART **I WAS THRILLED TO GET YOUR LETTER**

AND YES, WHAT A PLAN, JUST ME AND YOU
WE'LL RUN OFF TOGETHER, ELOPE TO PERU

PLUME: A nice idea, but Peru was never to be.
Part Four! Illicit doings in the gardens of the Smith country house at midnight.

Musicalised sex noises from MADELEINE and EMILE.

M & E: Oooo! Ahhh! Ow!

PLUME steps in swiftly to divert attention from this impropriety.

PLUME: For the full, un-expurgated, deeply improper correspondence, be sure not to miss...
Part Four!...

OF A PENNY DREADFUL STORY
NOW THE DEED IS DONE
A DASHING, DREADFUL FRENCHMAN
HER MAIDENHEAD IS WON
A PENNY DREADFUL STORY
A YOUNG GIRL LED ASTRAY
A PENNY DREADFUL STORY
WILL THEY RUE THE DAY?

MADELEINE: MY OWN BELOVED HUSBAND
IF WE DID WRONG LAST NIGHT
IT WAS IN THE EXCITEMENT OF OUR LOVE.

PLUME: Part Five! Her father finds out! Never contact my daughter again!

A moment as MADELEINE and EMILE try not to contact or think about each other. They struggle. They fail. They both reach for their pens... PING! notification on piano.

PLUME: Part Six! The engagement is back on.

MADELEINE: MY BEDROOM'S ON THE BOTTOM FLOOR
WITH RAILINGS JUST OUTSIDE
DROP A LETTER DOWN TO ME
(PRETEND YOUR SHOE NEEDS TIED)

He follows her instructions. Satisfied, they escalate.

SNEAK DOWN TO MY WINDOW
AND IN THE MIDNIGHT CHILL
I'LL BE WAITING WITH HOT COCOA
WOULDN'T WANT YOU GETTING ILL

MADELEINE is about to hand a cup to EMILE, but PLUME interrupts the actual drinking.

PLUME: Part seven! The introduction of a Mr William Minnoch, parentally-approved suitor for Madeleine. Can the affair with the Frenchman survive the arrival of a reputable suitor?

MADELEINE: EMILE,
MIGHT YOU MAYBE,
POSSIBLY
RETURN TO ME
MY LETTERS?

EMILE does not reply.

MADELEINE: MY LETTERS?

EMILE does not reply.

MADELEINE: I KNOW THAT AS A GENTLEMAN
YOU'LL OFFER NO REFUSAL

He realises gravity of this.

EMILE: I THINK I'LL SEND THEM ALL
TO YOUR FATHER FOR PERUSAL.

Her panic, then a change of approach.

MADELEINE: MY HUSBAND DEAR, MY ONLY LOVE
FORGIVE THY SILLY MIMI!
I'LL MAKE UP FOR THIS LITTLE ROW
WHEN YOU NEXT COME TO SEE ME.

PLUME: Part Eight! The purchase of the poison.

MADELEINE: *(practicing)* TWO PENN'ORTH OF THE POISON
FOR THE PANTRY WHERE THE PESTS ARE
TO ERASE THE WRETCHED RODENTS
(to self) NOW REMEMBER SUCH REQUESTS ARE
EVERYDAY AS EVERYONE
KNOWS ARSENIC IS BEST
TO BE RID OF WRETCHED RODENTS
WHEN YOUR PANTRY'S GOT A PEST

MADELEINE is in possession of the arsenic.

PLUME: Part Nine! The end of Emile!

EMILE: *(grandly)* WITH A BELLYFUL OF ARSENIC
I BID THIS LIFE ADIEU *(mispronounced)*

PLUME: *(correcting)* Adieu, surely?

EMILE dies.

MADELEINE: I PROMPTLY FLEE THE CITY
TO OUR COUNTRY HOUSE AT RHU

PLUME: HE'S BURIED, SHE'S ARRESTED,
A ROMANCE TURNED TO STRIFE,
SO NOW YOU KNOW WHY MADELEINE'S
ON TRIAL FOR HER LIFE!
IT'S A PENNY DREADFUL STORY
A GIRL FROM BLYTHSWOOD SQUARE

MEETS A DODGY FOREIGN FELLOW
HAS A CLANDESTINE AFFAIR
A PENNY DREADFUL STORY
NOW JUSTICE DOES ITS THING
A PENNY DREADFUL STORY
WILL SHE WALK OR WILL SHE SWING?

A warning to young ladies
Who get involved with men…

WE NOW AWAIT THE VERDICT,
SO STAY TUNED FOR PART TEN!

Suspense, drumroll moment.

P, M & E: The jury… by a majority… find a verdict of….

MADELEINE: Not Proven.

PLUME: AN UNCONCLUDED STORY
FIDDLY, TOO INVOLVED
FOR AN INDECISIVE JURY
WHO LEFT THE CASE UNSOLVED.
THIS UNIQUELY SCOTTISH VERDICT
CAN WE EVER KNOW WHAT'S TRUE?
INNOCENT OR GUITY?
WHAT'S A PAMPHLETEER…
A MID-VICTORIAN PAMPHLETEER…
A PENNY DREADFUL PAMPHLETEER…
TO DO?

PLUME: Not proven! Day after day in that sweltering court room, trial of the blasted century, all set to finish the series that puts my name (or at least my pseudonym) on the map, and… not proven? It's just not a proper verdict.

Underscore comes in.

Guilty, or not guilty, that's the way. Innocent until proven, of
course, but that's just it—until proven.

SONG 2: PLUME SONG

MY READERS WILL NOT STAND FOR IT,
THEY LIKE A TIDY END
I'VE NEVER MET A ONE OF THEM
BUT SOMEHOW THEY'RE MY FRIENDS
AND I HAVE GROWN TO LOVE MY LITTLE CLAQUE
MY JOB IS TO ENSURE THEY LOVE ME BACK
I STARTED WRITING PAMPHLETS
TO TELL TALES OF JUSTICE DONE
VILLAINS DON'T PREVAIL
THE GOOD HAVE ALWAYS WON
MURDERERS MUST MEET A RIGHTGEOUS
   DOOM
IF NOT, THEN WHAT'S THE POINT OF PLUME?

WHY PEDDLE TALES OF JUSTICE
IF THE WORLD WANTS ANARCHY?
IF MAD'LEINE SMITH CAN KILL A MAN
AND GET AWAY SCOT-FREE
THEN WHAT'S THE BLASTED POINT
   IN BEING GOOD?
IS THERE SOMETHING HERE THAT I'VE
   MISUNDERSTOOD?

I saw her.

PLUME summons MADELEINE.

My first murderess. My first time in a court room, actually. And I thought "this is it, I'm ready to experience life and write about life instead of just reading about it, and here I am in the public gallery of the case of cases!" Madeleine Smith, just 21 years old, her lover dead at her feet with a bellyful of arsenic...

EMILE *appears, falling at* MADELEINE's *feet.*

...and her with three entries in the poisons register for buying, what else? Arsenic. And yet here we are. Not. Proven.

Think, Plume, think! What are you going to say?

> I STARTED WRITING PAMPHLETS
> TO TELL TALES OF JUSTICE DONE
> VILLAINS DON'T PREVAIL
> THE GOOD HAVE ALWAYS WON
> MURDERERS MUST MEET A RIGHTEOUS DOOM
> IF NOT, THEN WHAT'S THE POINT OF PLUME?
> IF NOT, WHAT'S THE POINT /

MADELEINE: You could say that I'm innocent.

EMILE: That's a term nobody could, in good conscience, apply to you.

MADELEINE: I didn't ask for your opinion.

EMILE: You used to tell me you'd live by it.

MADELEINE: You used to tell me you loved me. We were both the more deceived.

PLUME: He's right, though. If you were innocent they'd have found you not guilty.

MADELEINE: If I were guilty they'd have hanged me.

PLUME: I can't say you're innocent.

MADELEINE: You can't say I'm guilty.

PLUME: But you killed him.

EMILE: You did kill me.

MADELEINE: Prove it.

PLUME: That's what I have to do! I have to prove it.

MADELEINE: You can't. The trial is over.

PLUME: Officially, yes. But 'not proven' is not an answer. There is an answer out there. I have to find it! And you two are going to help.

MADELEINE: I'm not.

PLUME: I'll have no backchat from my own imagination, thank you. I've been following this case since the very beginning, every step of the way, every sordid detail. If anyone can work out the truth, I can.

MADELEINE: You don't know any more than the jurors knew, and you're imagining us. How exactly do you think you're in a position to place me at the scene of the crime when the prosecution couldn't?

PLUME: Objection! You have a vested interest in talking me out of this!

MADELEINE: Even if you acquit me?

EMILE: C'est impossible.

MADELEINE: (to PLUME) Watch yourself around Emile. He's being more than usually French, that always means he wants something.

EMILE: All I want is justice, Mimi.

MADELEINE: Ugh, stop calling me that.

EMILE: Surely it benefits society as a whole to see my killer brought to justice?

PLUME: That's exactly my point!

MADELEINE: Then it's too late. Your killer's dead.

EMILE: I beg your pardo—

PLUME: What? Say more.

MADELEINE: (grabbing cuttings from PLUME's desk) Isn't it obvious? Look at this. Friends of Emile's describing him as a vain, foolish, morose man from Jersey who fancied himself French!

She steers PLUME over to a note pinned to the wall.

And this here—long before me, his affair with the mysterious 'Lady in Fife.' She jilts him, he threatens suicide. Maybe even attempts it. So when I told him it was over, what do you think he did?

EMILE: I did no such—

MADELEINE: But what if you did? And then left me on the hook for it?

PLUME: She's right, what if you did? Let me think...

As PLUME thinks this through, MADELEINE and EMILE act it out under his direction.

Emile's been hearing rumours about Madeleine and Mr Minnoch, a suitor chosen by her father—the father whose approval Emile could never win. She's been trying to avoid him, forcing him to threaten to reveal the affair! They meet.

MADELEINE: Emile, it's over.

EMILE: That's not how you spoke to me.

MADELEINE: I hate how I spoke to you.

EMILE: Accuracy is important.

MADELEINE: Ugh, if I must... My dearest Emile, my only love, there's nothing to be done. My father says I must wed Mr Minnoch. Our time is at an end, I beg you to understand. Forget thy Mimi and find a wife who can care for you as you deserve! Farewell forever!

SONG 3: EMILE'S LAMENT

EMILE: PRAY MOURN ME NOT, FORGET MY FATE
ANOTHER LOVE INVADES HER BREAST!
I NAME HER NOT, MY PARAMOUR
DESTROY THE LETTERS IN MY DESK!
IN MY DESK
IN MY DESK
THE LETTERS IN MY DESK
DANS LE BUREAU
DANS LE BUREAU
LES LETTRES DANS LE BUREAU
ADIEU!

PLUME coughs or raises eyebrow at pronunciation, which EMILE now corrects.

ADIEU!

He drinks.

AD—

PLUME cuts him off.

PLUME: Yes, yes, we get the idea. I can probably work with that. "Emile, scorned by his lover, dies by his own hand!" Or maybe "The missing letters! What secrets lay concealed in—"

MADELEINE: Trying to incriminate me! I burned all your letters, Emile. You could have done me the courtesy of doing the same.

EMILE: It's a cold soul who doesn't keep their love letters. But I meant what I said and nothing more. I hoped that some kind friend would destroy our correspondence and preserve your reputation.

MADELEINE: So ye did.

PLUME: I don't believe it anyway. I don't think that's what happened. Look!

> PLUME consults notes.

These letters that pass between them right at the end: "I think we shall be home on Tuesday, so I shall let you know, my own beloved sweet pet, when we shall have a dear, sweet interview" and "We shall speak of our union when we meet"—That doesn't sound like she's planning to break things off once and for all, does it? She must have been planning to carry on the affair. Buying herself more time? Intending to keep it going even after her marriage?

MADELEINE: What's that bit there?

PLUME: This bit? (*squints trying to make out handwriting*) That says Emile... arsenic... I think that's "white" and that's... oh!

> PLUME slams the notebook shut, mortified.

MADELEINE: "Stimulant" is what it says. Then in brackets, with a question mark—(she is about to say the word "sexual" but PLUME interrupts.)

PLUME: Miss Smith, please!

MADELEINE: What?

PLUME: It's not very becoming—

> MADELEINE laughs.

Well, it isn't! But I suppose it's a thought... The tone of her letters is much more fitting for... for that sort of rendez-vous. Well, we must consider it, I suppose. Let's take it from that night in the garden in Helensburgh.

MADELEINE: Rowaleyn is nowhere near Helensburgh, it's in Rhu.

EMILE: Which night exactly? There were so many.

PLUME: The first one, I assume. The one referred to here: "I think I would be wishing you to love me, if I were with you, but I don't suppose you would refuse me, for I know you will like to love your Mimi"—and the word "love" is underscored. Three times.

EMILE: Ah, of course. (*To MADELEINE*) Shall we?

They begin the scene.

MADELEINE: Again.

EMILE: (*groans*) Mimi, Emile est trop fatigué…

MADELEINE: Spoilsport.

EMILE: It's no easy thing to keep up with a young woman discovering the delights of passion for the first time.

MADELEINE: Who says it's the first time?

EMILE: You've had other lovers?

MADELEINE: I didn't say that. But I've felt it before. Every girl at school knew how to frig herself.

EMILE: Mimi!

PLUME: Miss Smith! I'm a pamphleteer, not a pornographer.

MADELEINE: What? You know how to excite yourself, surely?

PLUME: That is not the topic under discussion!

MADELEINE: It was that night. That's what I asked Emile.

PLUME: You know, I really think we should go back to looking at this as a love story, this is getting out of hand.

MADELEINE: I don't see why I'm getting told off for what you're imagining.

PLUME: Can we go back to your first meeting? There might be something I've missed, perhaps I misinterpreted—

MADELEINE: I think I made myself perfectly clear.

She picks up a letter.

"Some night soon I hope we may enjoy each other—I can fancy the first night we spend in each other's arms. If you were here now I am sure I would allow you to love me—I could not resist you." There's another one somewhere about letting him into my bedroom while I was in my nightgown. I'm sure you know where it is.

PLUME: Well, if you're going to cite references, look at all this— "my love, my own beloved Emile, my own dear fond husband my sweet." You must have been in love, surely?

MADELEINE: Yes, I thought that too. I was wrong. You know, they didn't read out all my letters in the courtroom. There were others. Worse ones. Letters you couldn't read in public. Shall I tell you what they said?

PLUME: Please, just get on with the scenario!

EMILE: (picking up where they left off) That's different.

MADELEINE: And you've actually had other lovers. There would be no point in a girl having a love affair with a dashing Frenchman who had no experience.

EMILE: You astonish me.

MADELEINE: Though if you can't keep up with me then perhaps I'll have to find myself another dashing Frenchman.

EMILE: (suddenly ice-cold and furious) Don't you dare say that. You can't ever belong to anyone else, do you understand? You're mine now.

MADELEINE: Emile, please! It was just a joke.

EMILE: After what we've just done no other man would want you anyway. If he knew. If anyone knew.

MADELEINE: But nobody needs to know because there's never going to be anyone but Emile. Don't be angry with me. I was only teasing.

EMILE: It's a perfect fascination, my attachment to you. Sometimes I have no idea why I should want you at all.

MADELEINE: Emile, husband, please...

EMILE: We shouldn't have done this. I can see that now. What if I were never to marry you?

MADELEINE: Don't say that! My own, my only love, I must be your wife! Only yours. You wouldn't disgrace your Mimi. Please. I could love no-one else.

EMILE: (suddenly warm again) Well, let's not fight. You made a bad joke, you won't do it again, we'll say no more about it. And next time we meet, so that I won't run the risk of disappointing the voracious Madame Mimi L'Angelier, I shall be certain to dose myself first.

MADELEINE: What?

> *Emile shows her bottle.*

MADELEINE: Copper ac-et-o-ars-en-ite.

> *[Chord]*

Why would you dose yourself with copper?

EMILE: That's not the active ingredient.

He whispers in her ear, chord as she hears, he's expecting a horrified reaction but doesn't get it.

MADELEINE: Oh, arsenic. I know it well, at school we used to—

EMILE: (not to be outdone) It's an element, that occurs naturally in the Earth's crust. And is also produced as a side-product of various industrial process such as smelting and the burning of coal. It's neither a metal nor a non-metal, but a metalloid. It's everywhere. It's in the wallpaper!

MADELEINE: What?

SONG 4: ARSENIC

EMILE:

IF YOU WANT YOUR WALLPAPER TO BE
  DARK GREEN
WHO DOESN'T WANT THEIR WALLPAPER TO BE
  DARK GREEN?
ARSENIC IS THE DYE
YOU REALLY NEED TO TRY
FOR THE DARKEST GREENEST WALLS YOU'VE
  EVER SEEN

IF YOU'RE INSTALLING WINDOW PANES YOU
  WANT STRONG GLASS
WHO WOULDN'T WANT THEIR WINDOW PANES
  TO HAVE STRONG GLASS?
YOU NEED GLASS THAT'S TOUGH
I KNOW JUST THE STUFF
USE GLASS THAT'S MIXED WITH ARESENIC
FOR WINDOWS THAT WILL LAST

THANK HEAVEN FOR ARESNIC
ATOMIC NUMBER THIRTY THREE
WALLPAPER AND WINDOWS
HALLELUJAH, GLORY BE!
THE KING OF POISONS AND THE POISON
  OF KINGS
IT'S USEFUL FOR SO MANY THINGS
ARSENIC'S YOUR LITTLE FRIEND
ARSENIC FOR ME!

M: IF YOU WANT YOUR SKIN TO BE SHINY AND
      BRIGHT

E: WHO WOULDN'T WANT THEIR SKIN TO BE
SHINY AND BRIGHT?

M: ARSENIC IS PERFECTION
IT'LL SORT OUT YOUR COMPLEXION
DILUTE IT, AND SCRUB IS ON YOUR FACE
IN THE MORNING AND AT NIGHT

M AND E: THANK HEAVEN FOR ARESNIC
ATOMIC NUMBER THIRTY THREE
SKIN THAT'S BRIGHT AND SHINY
HALLELUJAH, GLORY BE!
THE KING OF POISONS AND THE POISON
  OF KINGS
IT'S USEFUL FOR SO MANY THINGS
A SPOTTY SCHOOLGIRL'S LITTLE FRIEND
ARSENIC FOR ME!

E: It's used as a wood preservative

M: TO KEEP YOUR FENCE FROM ROT

E: It's used by ceramacists

M: TO MAKE A MORE DURABLE POT

M & E: IT'S USED IN MAKING BULLETS
TO MAKE THEM HARD WITHIN
AND TAXIDERMISTS USE IT
FOR PRESERVING ANIMAL SKIN

E: MY ROSES ARE COVERED IN INSECTS
THEY REALLY ARE A PEST
AND I SAW A RAT IN THE KITCHEN

M: YOU KNOW WHAT I SUGGEST?

M & E: IT'S THE KING OF POISONS AND
             THE POISON OF KINGS
          IT'S USEFUL FOR SO MANY THINGS
          ARSENIC'S YOUR LITTLE FRIEND
          ARSENIC FOR ME!

Dance break.

E: A FEW GRAINS OF ARSENIC

M: (*warning*) JUST A LITTLE BIT

E: HELPS ME WITH MY STAMINA, I'M HAPPY
          TO ADMIT
          IF I GET THE DOSE JUST RIGHT
          IT KEEPS ME UP ALL NIGHT
          SWALLOW DOWN THE ARSENIC
          AND WAIT FOR THE HIT

M AND E: THANK HEAVEN FOR ARESNIC
          ATOMIC NUMBER THIRTY THREE
          IT KEEPS ME / YOU UP ALL NIGHT
          HALLELUJAH, GLORY BE!
          THE KING OF POISONS AND THE POISON
             OF KINGS
          IT'S USEFUL FOR SO MANY THINGS
          ARSENIC'S YOUR LITTLE FRIEND
          SO MANY WAYS IT CAN BE APPLIED
          WALLPAPER AND INSECTICIDE
          ARSENIC'S YOUR LITTLE FRIEND
          GOOD FOR YOUR COMPLEXION
          HELP WITH YOUR ERECTION
          ARSENIC'S YOUR LITTLE FRIEND
          ARSENIC FOR ME!

EMILE: You can never have too much of a good thing!

MADELEINE: Measure carefully, mind! See you at midnight on the... (*she checks PLUME's letters*) ...7th!

They part.

SONG 5a: **WAITING #1** (EMILE'S ACCIDENTAL OVERDOSE)

MADELEINE: MIDNIGHT! COME TO ME, MY LOVE!

EMILE: MIDNIGHT! I COME TO YOU, MY LOVE!

EMILE takes the poison, all set for a busy night. He takes a little extra for good measure...

MADELEINE waits.

EMILE dies.

The clock strikes one.

MADELEINE: IT SEEMS HE'S BEEN DELAYED
            DID I HAVE THE RIGHT DAY?

Clock strikes two.

            I WANT TO END THIS SONG
            BEFORE I REALISE SOMETHING'S
            WRONG

MADELEINE: Please. I don't want to relive it. Worrying all night, waking up to learn of Emile's sudden, accidental death...

PLUME: How tragic!

MADELEINE: Isn't it? And you thought I killed him. Just imagine what I've been through.

PLUME: You poor thing! What a headline— "Heartbroken beauty tried for the crime of falling in—"

EMILE: Except that's not what happened, is it? It wasn't accidental was it? There was still the matter of her other fiancé. She still had motive.

PLUME: Ah. Yes.

MADELEINE: Motive doesn't get 240 grains of arsenic into a man's stomach without him noticing. There's no way—

PLUME: But what if there was? I think I have it— go back to where you were.

MADELEINE and EMILE take their positions from the end of the duet.

No no, earlier— at the beginning.

MADELEINE: The whole thing again? Really?

EMILE: It does seem like unnecessary repetition.

PLUME: Just mark it!

With a bit of grumbling MADELEINE and EMILE fast-forward through the Arsenic song and the Midnight moment.

PLUME: Stop there! Now Emile takes his dose like he said.

EMILE takes his dose of the poison.

MADELEINE: And what's my role in all this?

PLUME: You're going to take some of the poison you bought and boil it up in the cocoa.

MADELEINE: Why, exactly?

PLUME: To make him sick! So he won't see your engagement notice in the papers!

MADELEINE: This seems like a very short-term plan...

PLUME: You're desperate, all right? He's going to send all your letters to your father if you don't stop him somehow. No-one is saying it's a good plan, just that it's a plan. Now if I may?

PLUME puts them into position and cues them. MADELEINE waits for EMILE, mixing up the cocoa, stirring in the poison.

SONG 5b: **WAITING #2** (EMILE'S ASSISTED OVERDOSE)

MADELEINE: NOT ENOUGH TO KILL A MAN,
JUST A LITTLE HELPING HAND
WASN'T THAT WHAT WE HAD PLANNED?
HANDLE THIS, LOVE, IF YOU CAN…

EMILE arrives, chilled, accepts the poisoned cocoa, goes to embrace MADELEINE, has sudden violent pain. SILENT MELODRAMA. EMILE dies. MADELEINE watches.

PLUME: There, you see? "Secrets, stamina, sordid assignations! How a cocoa-fuelled carnal tryst turned toxic!" You both killed him! That's why there was so much arsenic in his stomach! He took some for… stamina, she gave him some to make him sick so he wouldn't see the news of her engagement, and altogether it was lethal!

MADELEINE: I think you read too many novels.

EMILE: It does seem a bit far-fetched.

PLUME: I don't believe you two really care about figuring out the truth.

MADELEINE: I'm trying to be helpful! I gave you the Emile suicide theory, didn't I? And you dismissed it because you're determined that nobody could have killed him but me.

EMILE: Everyone thinks that.

MADELEINE: The jury didn't.

EMILE: Then why didn't they say not guilty? I'll tell you why— it's because all of them either know your father or would like to know your father, and they're not going to risk making an enemy of him by hanging his daughter.

MADELEINE: My trial stood on its own merits, it had nothing to do with—

EMILE: If you'd been from a poor family you'd be preparing to answer to your maker for your crimes at this moment.

MADELEINE: If I'd been from a poor family you'd never have looked at me in the first place.

EMILE: That's true.

PLUME: Monsieur L'Angelier! Such a thing to admit!

EMILE: Marrying well is a time-honoured tradition. It's no different to Madeleine's intention to marry William Minnoch.

MADELEINE: Mr Minnoch's social standing is the least a girl from my background should be—

EMILE: You see? One rule for the rich, another for the likes of me! That's the true death sentence— the one a man pays for getting above his station!

SONG 6: JERSEY BOY

JERSEY'S A PLACE YOU DON'T ASK TO BE BORN
IF YOU WANT TO CLIMB OUT OF POVERTY'S
  TRENCH
YOU'RE STUCK IN BETWEEN, YOU'VE NO
  ENGLISH PRIDE
AND DON'T EVEN GET TO BE FRENCH.
WHAT'S TO BE DONE FOR A MAN WHO'S STILL
  YOUNG
AND FEELS THE WING'D CHARIOT HARD AT HIS
  BACK?
WHEN WORK'S A DEAD END BUT YOU'VE STILL
  GOT YOUR LOOKS?
FIND A WIFE TO PROVIDE ME WITH ALL THAT
  I LACK.

IF I FIND THE RIGHT WIFE THEN THE REST OF
    MY LIFE
THERE'LL ALWAYS BE FOOD ON THE TABLE
JUDGE IF YOU WILL, IT'S SOCIETY'S ILL
I'M TAKING THE CHANCE WHILE I'M ABLE

JERSEY'S A PLACE YOU DON'T ASK TO BE BORN
IT'S WEARISOME HAVING TO FILL UP ONE'S
    CUP
I'VE TRIED THE RIGHT WAY, IT JUST DOESN'T
    PAY
SO WHAT'S WRONG WITH MARRYING UP?

PLUME: I think I see now why your father didn't approve.

MADELEINE: Shocking isn't it? Surprising that no one considered him as a suspect?

PLUME: You mean...

MADELEINE: Why not? Look...

MADELEINE sets the scene, waiting for her appointment with EMILE as before. The clock strikes 12.

SONG 7: **WAITING # 3** (HER FATHER DID IT)

MADELEINE: MIDNIGHT! COME TO ME MY LOVE!

Clock srikes one.

THEN I SEE A MAN—NOT EMILE, BUT MY
    FATHER
HIS MANNER'S DETERMINED, AND I THINK I'D
    RATHER
NOT KNOW WHERE HE'S BEEN, OR WHAT'S
    DONE,
OR WHO'S—NO!

IN THE MORNING I'LL KNOW WHAT I DON'T WANT TO KNOW.

For a moment MADELEINE lingers in the image of innocence, watching for PLUME's reaction.

EMILE: An entertaining idea, but even harder to prove. As much as I requested introductions to Madeleine's father, there's no evidence that I ever got one and it's difficult to be poisoned by a man whose acquaintance one has never made.

MADELEINE: Almost as difficult as it is to marry his daughter. It's a hard world for fortune-hunters.

EMILE: There had to be some explanation for my fascination for you.

MADELEINE: I understand that now. (*To PLUME*) What I don't understand is yours. Why are you so obsessed with me?

PLUME: I'm not.

MADELEINE: You are. You and your readers and everyone who was crowded round the court today waiting for the verdict. The warden had to sneak me out the back door, the streets were so busy. But first they found a young woman who had been hanging around every day hoping for a glimpse of me and they asked if she'd be my decoy. She didn't even look like me, but... coal scuttle bonnet, handkerchief held to the face, she'd do. And of course they dressed her in my clothes. That's why she agreed to do it. Willing to risk being torn to shreds by an angry mob as long as I let her keep the dress. It's a pity. I liked that dress. Perhaps it brought me luck. Would you have done it, if they'd asked?

PLUME: I—I don't—

MADELEINE: You don't have to answer. I can guess.

PLUME: It's just— it's fascinating, that's all. There's never been a trial quite like it.

EMILE: True. The women who stand trial for murder are usually poor. It's surprising that the exquisite Miss Smith ever made it to court.

MADELEINE: Emile, do you have to be so dreary? This is why everyone thinks you're a fortune hunter, because you never shut up about this stuff. "Ah, pauvre moi, your father despises me because I'm poor, you don't really love me because I'm poor, pauvre Emile and all his terrible problemes." You know why my father really didn't like you? Because he thought you were manipulating me.

EMILE: As if anyone could ever have manipulated you!

MADELEINE: You gave it a damn good try though! Here!

She snatches letters from PLUME's desk/notes from the walls.

"You have deceived your father as you have deceived me. You never told him how solemnly you bound yourself to me, or if you had, for the honour of his daughter he could not have asked to break off an engagement like ours. Think what your father would say if I sent him your letters for a perusal."

'I am sad at what you did, I regret it very much. Why, Mimi, did you give way after your promises? I do not understand, my pet, your not bleeding for every woman having her virginity must bleed.'

You never kept copies of any of your other letters, just these few.

If I didn't poison you, perhaps I should have.

SONG 8: WHEN A GIRL SAYS NO

MADELEINE: WHEN A GIRL SAYS NO
THERE'S NO MORE TO SAY
LOVE'S GONE AWAY
YOU'VE LOST YOUR PREY, IT'S OVER

WHEN A GIRL SAYS NO
THAT'S WHEN YOU LET HER GO.
WHEN A GIRL SAYS NO
YOU HAVE TO LET IT END
DO YOU COMPREHEND?
SHE'S NOT YOUR FRIEND, IT'S OVER
WHEN A GIRL SAYS NO
THAT'S WHEN YOU LET HER GO

MAYBE I'M NOT INNOCENT
BUT WHY SHOULD I FEEL GUILT?
YOU BOARDED UP THE EXITS
FROM THIS MADHOUSE THAT WE BUILT
YOU TRAPPED ME IN YOUR FANTASY
DROWNED MY MIND IN DOUBT
NOW KILLING YOU'S THE ONLY WAY
I'M EVER GETTING OUT

TWO PENN'ORTH OF THE POISON
FOR PANTRY WHERE THE PESTS ARE

YOU PLANNED TO USE ME
AND LEAVE ME THE REGRET
DON'T YOU KNOW A TELL-TALE
RISKS THE PUNISHMENT THEY GET
THE GIRL I WAS?
I DIDN'T LIE
SHE'S YOURS AND YOU CAN KEEP HER
THE NEW ME WEARS HER SKIN
AND LEAVES THE OLD HER TO THE REAPER
YOU TARGETED A TEENAGE GIRL
YOU SHOULD HAVE DIED OF SHAME
I'LL RE-INVENT MYSELF SO HARD

THE WORLD WON'T KNOW MY NAME
WON'T KNOW MY NAME!

MAYBE I'M NOT INNOCENT
BUT WHY SHOULD I FEEL SHAME
YOU BOARDED UP THE EXITS
FROM THIS MADHOUSE THAT WE BUILT
YOU TRAPPED ME IN YOUR FANTASY
DROWNED MY MIND IN DOUBT
NOW KILLING YOU'S THE ONLY WAY
I HAD OF GETTING OUT

EMILE lies dead at MADELEINE's feet.

PLUME: I don't know how to make a headline out of that. "Roué pays the price of ill-advised affair?" "A Glasgow girl's revenge?" "He had it coming?" It doesn't sit right with the rest of the series. I can't encourage young ladies to go around poisoning people.

MADELEINE: Not even if it saves them from ruin?

PLUME: But it hasn't saved you from ruin! You are ruined!

MADELEINE: Am I? I have the rest of my life to live. I might go to London. Or New York, maybe. I can start again.

PLUME: Surely not. Everyone knows who you are, what you did—

MADELEINE: What I might have done. All they know for certain is that I'm not the pure, innocent girl they'd like to take home to meet Mother. I'm free from that, at least.

I might not know what I'll do next, but I know that I won't be hanged, I won't stifle myself playing the ingenue, and I won't tell. Ever. So now you know that you'll never know. What's to become of your precious pamphlet?

PLUME: I think I'm going to stick to the version I had in mind. "Madeleine escapes the noose."

MADELEINE: Really? We've been through all this and you're still going to portray me as a straightforward murderer who got away with it?

PLUME: I'm sorry. It's just that all the complex stuff, all the possibilities... they won't sell. Would you buy a pamphlet about a society belle who maybe poisoned her lover but equally maybe didn't? My readers are going to want an angle. I'll add what ambiguity I can.

MADELEINE: Brave of you to incur my anger when you've seen what happens to those who do.

PLUME: I can only dream.

MADELEINE: What?

PLUME: It would be an honour to be murdered by you.

MADELEINE: That's... not what I expected. Weren't you wanting me to hang?

PLUME: You should. If you killed him. And I really think you might have done.

MADELEINE: But you're glad I did.

PLUME: I didn't say that.

MADELEINE: And I didn't say I did it.

PLUME: But if you had, that makes you the most famous, the most talked about, the most... glamourous of murderers.

MADELEINE: To die at my hands would be glamourous, then?

PLUME: It would be something.

MADELEINE: Find another reason to be talked about, you parasocial little fiend. Now, I've spent enough time being imagined by you. Let me out of your grubby little head.

PLUME: Just as soon as I have my headline.

MADELEINE: Well, what about this? "Not Proven: Madeleine Smith escapes the noose, but she'll never escape Emile."

EMILE: You killed me! How much more of an escape—

MADELEINE: And yet you're still here! And this is how it's always going to be, Madeleine and Emile forever and ever, picked at, pored over, wondered about! THAT is my real sentence, and I don't know whether I deserve it or not.

MADELEINE rests her hand on the MUSICIAN's shoulder, every inch the perfect Victorian girl as she steals the scene from PLUME and begins the end.

SONG 10: SOMETHING IN BETWEEN

MADELEINE: I DON'T OWE YOU RESOLUTION

PLUME: (*spoken*) But I've got to have an ending!

MADELEINE: YOU'VE NO RIGHT TO MY ORDEAL

PLUME: (*spoken*) The world has a right to know!

MADELEINE: I DON'T HAVE TO TELL MY STORY

PLUME: (*spoken*) Maybe not, but I have to—

MADELEINE: I DON'T CARE HOW YOU FEEL

PLUME: (*spoken*) You've made that abundantly clear!

EMILE take a breath, about to sing.

MADELEINE: (*spoken*) Shut up, Emile.
I DON'T OWE YOU MY REPENTANCE
FOR WHAT I DID OR DIDN'T DO
I DON'T HAVE TO SAY WE'RE SORRY
OR RELIVE WHAT WE WENT THROUGH

PLUME desperately tries to wrest control of the scene from MADELEINE.

PLUME: IT'S A PENNY DREADFUL STORY

MADELEINE: YOU CAN ONLY SPECULATE
ON WHAT MIGHT HAVE BEEN

PLUME: TELLING TALES OF MURDER IS MY SPECIALITY

MADELEINE: I JUST CONTROL MY ACTIONS
NOT THE WAY I'M SEEN
THERE'S INNOCENCE, AND THERE'S GUILT
AND THEN THERE'S SOMETHING IN BETWEEN.

LA LA LA LA   LA LA LA LA
LA LA LA LA   LA LA LA LA

YOU MIGHT READ WHAT WE'VE WRITTEN
BUT YOU CAN'T KNOW WHAT WE MEAN
THERE'S INNOCENCE AND THERE'S GUILT
AND THERE'S SOMETHING IN BETWEEN.
THERE'S INNOCENCE AND THERE'S GUILT
AND WE ALL LIVE IN BETWEEN.

PLUME, spiralling, dismisses MADELEINE and EMILE. He tries to regain control. It's not a successful attempt.

PLUME: I STARTED WRITING PAMPHLETS
TO TELL TALES OF JUSTICE DONE
I THOUGHT I'D DEAL IN SIMPLE FACTS
MY FORTE'S CLEAR COMMUNICATION
NOT COMPLEX INTERPRETATION
THIS SHOULD HAVE GONE A CERTAIN WAY
WHAT IF THEY DON'T LIKE WHAT I SAY?
WHO WANTS A BLOODY MYSTERY?
IF I CAN'T GIVE YOU CERTAINTY
IF I'M NOT WHAT YOU WANT FROM ME
THEN THE THE HELL'S THE POINT OF ME
IF I DON'T KNOW WHAT I BELIEVE
YOU'LL THINK I'M YOUNG AND JUST NAÏVE
I HAVE TO TELL YOU WHAT IS WHAT

As the following lines repeat, the MUSICIAN discreetly leaves the stage, abandoning PLUME to his own mind.

IT'S EITHER PROVEN OR IT'S NOT
IT'S EITHER PROVEN OR IT'S NOT
IT'S EITHER PROVEN OR IT'S NOT
IT'S—

PLUME stares out at the audience, desperate for their love and approval.

I don't know what to say because what I want to say is *I don't know* but I don't know whether you'll still love me if I say I don't know and I don't know if I can—don't know what to—I don't know how to not know.

How do you know how not to know?

Lights out on PLUME.

THE END.

ALSO AVAILABLE FROM SALAMANDER STREET

All Salamander Street plays can be bought in bulk at a discount for performance or study. Contact info@salamanderstreet.com to enquire about performance licenses.

A PLAY, A PIE AND A PINT: VOLUME ONE
ISBN: 9781913630225

6 plays from Òran Mór including *Toy Plastic Chicken* by Uma Nada-Rajah, *A Respectable Widow takes to Vulgarity* by Douglas Maxwell, *Chic Murray: A Funny Place for a Window* by Stuart Hepburn, *Ida Tampson* by Denise Mina, *Jocky Wilson Said* by Jane Livingstone and Jonathan Cairney, *Do Not Press This Button* by Alan Bissett

A PLAY, A PIE AND A PINT: VOLUME TWO
8 One-Act Plays from Òran Mór.
ISBN: 9781068696237

To celebrate the beloved Glasow theatrical institution's 20th anniversary, this second collection includes critically acclaimed plays and favourites as voted by the public and members of the theatre company.

PLACEHOLDER by Catherine Bisset
ISBN: 9781068696282

A parallel text version of Catherine Bisset's dramatic solo play set in 1790 Saint-Domingue – the daughter of an enslaved woman reflects on her life as an opera singer and the importance of resistance.

THE CHING ROOM & TURBO FOLK
by Alan Bissett
ISBN: 9781913630997

A pitch-black two-hander set in a toilet cubicle, and a sharp look at Scottish nationality at home and abroad.

O IS FOR HOOLET by Ishbel McFarlane
ISBN: 9781913630126

A solo show about the Scots language that challenges and disrupts our expectations and prejudices about language.